Dear Friend… with Benefits

Bianca Perrie

For those who know what it is to not know what it is.

II

Dear Friend... with Benefits,

I thought you

would be my next love,

and that my next love,

would be my great love,

but here's what I got instead...

Number One: I Got... A One Night stand.

I met you

like an accident.

And not some

raging six-car crash

on a stormy September night,

no,

more like a paper cut

from reaching out too quickly.

By accident.

By some small, minute,

accident,

I met you.

We met as a consequence

of sharing the same friends.

We met as a consequence

of being the last two people

in the same room

together at a party.

We met as a consequence

of my inability

to stand silence

and your ability

to speak to anyone.

I saw you earlier,

but I didn't lust after you.

I didn't even think about you

in a sexual way.

Until you opened

your mouth.

The motion of your

full lips forming

made the ground beneath

my feet feel

unsteady.

Your voice

flowed like honey;

sweet and slow,

smooth and thick,

and satisfying.

It made me lightheaded.

But also,

I had mixed dark rum

and cognac

and tequila

in the same red solo cup.

A poisonous concoction

that was sure

to make me act up –

and out of character.

I'd never done anything

like this in my life.

My senses were

simultaneously

heightened and dulled,

like the edges of an old knife.

You caught me

with my guard down.

You caught me in

a moment of metamorphosis.

I was shedding

who I used to be.

I was open

to the idea

of living my life

with you

for one night.

I'd never

allowed myself

to open up

to a stranger.

I was a chamber of secrets,

a vault of private experiences.

I thought these thoughts

and I thought these locks

were impenetrable;

that's because

I'd never let them be,

they could never be free.

But you had a masterful key

and you unlocked me.

I've never allowed myself

to be reckless.

The recklessness,

granted,

was borne,

out of drunkenness.

The irony of it all

is that this liquid

gave me the courage to be

who I was too frightened to be

and that was a sobering thing.

My judgement was clouded

according to the legal alcohol limit,

but pivot,

my judgement turned to action

according to the laws of attraction.

I mean,

the more you spoke to me,

the more my attraction to you grew.

I loved the way

your mind worked.

I loved the way

the thoughts formed

in your brain

and the order in which

these words flew

out of your mouth.

I followed your mind map

everywhere,

every direction you led us in,

I never detoured.

When you told me

about your love for waffles,

I was certain,

I'd never be the girl for you.

It may sound silly,

but I was more of a

pancake person.

Sure,

they were both golden and fluffy,

but one had the power to deceive –

pancakes appeared as they were.

Soft and truthful.

Waffles looked crunchy,

especially the gourmet ones,

but then,

one bite into it,

and it's a cloud on your tongue.

Despite being worth the risk,

waffles were deceptive.

Who could trust a waffle person?

Knowing you were

a waffle person

and I was a pancake person

and knowing this difference

meant that all we had

was tonight,

I plotted

to make my move.

What would be

the most effective approach

in getting to you?

I've got bar graphs

and pie charts

forming in my head.

I've got histograms

and timeplots

calculating

how to get you into bed.

I know

I shouldn't really

make it this complex,

but where does

your Y meet my X?

As the heat in my body

gradually grows...

As my pulse

increases incrementally...

I send you signals.

Are we connecting?

I realize we're on the same page

when you bite your lip...

when your pupils dilate...

when you lean into me...

And when the front

of your grey sweatpants bulge,

I read you like a book.

I lean in,

closing the galactic gap

between us.

The tension

between us

is like shooting stars,

balls of fire,

so hot,

we compete with the sun.

If I could wish on these stars,

I'd waste it.

I'd wish for what I already have.

I'd wish for you.

I taste your lips

and I let you taste mine.

There's a primal hunger,

akin to a predator

pouncing on its prey,

except,

we are both the hunters,

out in the wilderness,

weapons cocked and loaded.

Who will fire first?

You excuse yourself

without reason.

And the 60 seconds of abandonment

rips into me:

> OH, WILL THOU LEAVE ME SO
>
> UNSATISFIED?

You finally return

and you return with news

of an empty room downstairs.

Oh.

Oh!

On a lumpy little bed,

I call out your name –

a name I've only just learned –

a name I would soon forget.

A name.

It's unimportant.

It's inconsequential.

It pales in comparison

to the names of the things

we are doing to each other.

We are making music,

rocking each other's worlds.

Oh, *oh.*

Even as shame

and guilt

and regret

attempt to creep in,

your body keeps them at bay.

For a single moment,

we share the same anchor

in a sea of desire.

Two decent people…

Two decent souls…

must there be more?

Your essence ripples through me.

First,

an ebbing lake,

then,

an oceanic wave.

If all one-night stands

were like this,

then this is all there would be.

Number Two: I Got... a Second Time Planned.

The unexpected

Ding!

of an iMessage

jolts me from my daydream.

Hey Miss.

Three days too late,

and yet,

earlier than the never

I had expected.

I stare at your number

at the top of the screen,

recalling how

we'd exchanged many things,

but believing numbers

weren't one of them.

It reads,

Maybe: You

and it feels like

a question I can't answer.

I play it honest.

I reply.

This is a surprise.

Like reaching in and finding

there's actually two cookies

left in the jar.

Like having your extensive tab

taken care of

at a shmoozy bar.

Like learning your credit score

is finally up to par.

A surprise.

A wonderful surprise.

I should've said wonderful.

I watch and I wait

as those three mysterious dots

appear and disappear

as you decide

what to say next.

Those three dots –

the ellipses –

I have always wondered about that.

The ellipses

and the trailing off thought.

The ellipses

and the omission of thought.

The ellipses

and... *Ding!*

You reply:

You going to that mansion party Saturday?

When.

When I see you on Saturday,

I will have so many questions.

When we both arrive,

will we greet each other

like people who have shared bodies?

What?

What will you say

when you see me?

What will you think of me with

sober eyes, sober ears,

and a sober heart?

What will you think of me

then, there, at a place

where you expect to see me?

Where?

Where is this going?

Where do I need it to go?

Why?

Why do you care

about my presence at a place?

If we've never

appeared at the same party prior

to this one,

then why should this

be any different?

Who?

And who will you be

the next time we meet?

Are you a man

looking for another easy lay

or are you a man

ready to sweep me off my feet

and carry me away?

Maybe: You.

Appears at the top of my screen

again.

Maybe we can meet up after?

I type: *Yes.*

Period and all,

the tone of that text

carries a confidence

and a certainty

I cannot bring myself to feel.

But Maybe: You

doesn't reply right away.

Maybe: You

responds a day late.

Maybe: You

says *Sounds great.*

And I find myself dissecting this.

S for... Saturday.

Which is fitting.

It's the best day of the week.

It's the do-nothing

or do-everything

day of the week.

And I'm sure you can guess

which one I think best.

Saturday when I see you,

sexier than

what I seemed to summon up

in my psyche.

O for... Open.

The layout of the party

was as open as the lake it

looked out onto.

As open as the day is long.

As open as my legs would be.

Open-hearted, open-minded,

opting for the opportunity to

optimize being in your omnipresence.

U for… Unfair.

It is unfair

how unequally matched we are.

When our eyes meet

over top an upholstered sofa,

I have to hold my breath.

It is unfair

the ubiquitous universe

brought you to me

under the assumption

I could handle you.

N for… Need.

As soon as I see you,

I need you.

The need is immediate,

for the night is short.

And we have many things to catch up on,

many needs to meet.

A naive neophyte

to this kind of need,

but neurotic and nocturnal,

the need is noteworthy.

D for… Dance.

When I'm wining on you

to warm R&B beats,

I've discovered another way

our bodies are in tandem.

The dancing doubles my desire

and your discursive double-entendres

disparage my defenses.

S for... Situation.

A circumstance

we've found ourselves in,

indeed,

a situation.

It palpitates with promise.

And I swear,

tonight,

there is no circumstance,

no surrounding,

no state I'd rather stand in,

soon to be skin-to-skin.

G for... Gentleman.

The way you

politely conduct yourself,

doling out drinks for others,

opening doors for others,

cleaning up after others –

I'm more attracted to you for this,

but what about me?

Genteel Gentleman,

go.

To goad me is grotesque.

Grovel grandiose,

good gentleman.

R for… Ready.

Yes,

I'm ready to go.

You don't ask this with words,

but with your eyes.

Regale me with risqué regard.

Our ruse restarts.

E for… Echo.

The sounds of you

reverberate through me,

again and again;

they're trapped in me.

Ensnared,

engulfed,

and entertained,

I am.

I embrace you and your effervescence.

A for... Adventure.

I accept your offer

and I accept the adventure

we're going to go on,

for as long as we're going

to go on it.

We attend an area

alas all alone,

and as admirers –

all apparel away!

T for time.

It didn't take much time

for us to find our way

to an empty bedroom,

and here we are,

for the second time.

It's strange

how you do not feel

like a stranger inside of me.

My one night stand

becomes a two-night stand

and I can't stand myself

for not understanding that

Maybe we can meet up after?

was a proposition for this grandstand.

And I'm sorry

if I'm coming off

a little standoffish –

Even though,

I'm the one

to make that which

is taboo standard,

I'm usually more of a bystander

and that's the truth,

notwithstanding.

And this second night with you

was outstanding.

Number Three: I Got... More.

When the post-sex texting

never stopped,

I bought in,

like a gambler

at the racetrack,

all bets were on.

I wanted to be all in.

Some days,

I thought I was.

Some days,

you made me feel

lucky to be alive,

lucky to be in your presence,

lucky to intimately know you.

Other days,

something was missing,

something caused my eye to wander,

something I knew I had to find

in someone else.

But you caught onto this.

Often and always.

With all your experience,

you ran circles around me.

If it were a competition,

you'd be the racehorse

to put money on,

because when you smiled at me,

when you were all in too,

I never stood a chance.

If there were winners and losers,

you were always in first place

and never made me feel

like I came last.

But if there's a winner,

surely,

too,

there must be a loser.

And so,

if my interest waned

and your access to the tracks

became limited,

you'd step up –

an extra compliment,

a tiny gift,

a loving gesture.

How could I not buy in?

And just when I thought

I knew exactly what this was

and would be,

you changed the rules.

You asked me out on a date.

By text –

of course.

A simple one liner.

A question.

Like you didn't just

set off a bomb

in our peaceful little village.

But as we both know,

under the circumstances,

I am at your mercy.

Yes,

I reply,

with trembling

and unsure fingers.

My nervous system

stays in shock

the days leading up

to seeing you again.

It's like all the times before

times a million more.

Nerves.

Because this time

means something different,

I think.

This time,

you want to know

if you can love me

beyond the bedroom.

Whether I believe it or not

is inconsequential.

No one

ever wants the answer

to that question

to be

no.

So we go,

and we connect –

our minds instead of our bodies –

and we laugh,

and we empathize,

and we become more

than what we were.

And on that first date,

showing chinks in your armour:

I am wounded, you see,

but you can have what's left of me.

I want to know

the reasons behind every battle scar,

every purple bruise,

every 'I will smile

but I won't let myself

relax with you.'

I want you

to let down your guard,

remove your armor

and show me your sword.

Because I am weapon-less.

I cannot hurt you.

And I will not.

In fact,

did I ever tell you

my brother is a welder?

And I may have picked up

a thing or two.

I can melt

and mend

and hammer

and repair

every dent if you let me.

For some reason,

my reassurance is not

a big enough shove.

And still,

you are only brave enough

to remove your gloves.

But progress is progress

and I will take what I can get,

because you are

a knight in shining armor

even though

you don't know it yet.

So I push

and I push

and I push

'til you crack.

And I wait

for the shards

to come flying back.

Because every action

has an opposite

and equal reaction.

Instead,

you surprise me.

Like a twist ending

in a newly released movie.

You remove your helmet

and show me your eyes –

the windows to your soul,

and yes,

the pain is visible.

You proceed to tell me

about Cinderella #1...

only she never

made it to the ball.

You tell me about

Cinderella #2...

who took all of your riches

and never returned a call.

You tell me about

Cinderella #3...

whose foot fit perfectly

in the glass slipper,

only she found

that the shoes

that your best friend

owned were better.

I stop you

just before you tell me about

Cinderella #4

because these previous patterns

don't matter anymore –

I am here.

I don't know

how long

I will be here,

but I am here.

I am not

out to get you,

to let you down,

to take from you,

or to deceive you.

I cannot say

what I do not feel.

I want to know you,

yes –

I want to comfort you,

of course.

I want to

bring you a peace

that those before me

could not.

But as you do not ask

more of me,

I cannot ask this either.

So you lower your head.

When I place my hand

on the small of your back,

you let out a sigh

and I catch something

in your eyes.

Something in your eyes

shines brighter

than the stars.

And the space

between you and I

seems a little less far.

So, I have to try.

I try to tell you –

I see the good parts of you.

I champion the parts of you

that need more.

More kindness,

more attention,

more love.

Sir skyscraper,

I build you up.

Still you keep me

at a distance.

Just as I throw my hands up

frustrated by your resistance,

you surprise me.

You reach for my hand

(though you are

already holding my heart).

You trace

your body

with my palms,

and my heart

(the one that you

are holding)

begins to tick

like a bomb.

Tick, tick.

Just looking at you,

no one would know

you were carrying

so much weight –

with my hands on you,

I realize it is never too late.

Tick, tick.

With my hands on you,

you let me remove

your chest plate.

Tick, tick.

You stand before me:

bare and beautiful.

You tell me,

take all the metal,

my protection,

and my suit –

I no longer need it

because I trust in you.

Boom.

For an ephemeral moment

in time,

we are more.

Number Four: I Got… Less.

Now.

Now that we have sex,

and we date,

and we talk

every day –

and you know the things,

all the things,

things I could barely

admit to myself –

secrets.

Secrets seems too simple

a word

for what you know –

now.

You know me now.

Somehow,

we are in-between,

now.

Not quite couple,

but beyond friends.

This stage called

"talking"

is a mystery

and a thriller to me.

I never know

what to expect,

what outing,

what conversations,

what introductions

are coming next.

This is thriller.

The thrill only adds

to the sexual chemistry

that is alight

every time

we are together.

But when we are not

together,

the time is

shrouded in mystery.

It's misery.

Up and down,

but I continue

to stick around.

We talk

you like to say –

but it seems to me,

we don't talk –

at least

not about

the biggest thing

of all.

And you know

that I am invested,

you know.

You know what

I have my sights

set on.

If the investment was

betting at race tracks

before,

it's become something

much more.

I'm in it now,

you know.

It's long-term pay off,

it's 401K,

it's pension.

It's a sizeable pay-in,

but I put my stocks at stake.

You know what

I have my sights

set on.

On.

On a mountain peak,

we're at a point,

in which no man

can stand on

forever.

Forever –

we have to talk

about forever and us,

or forever but us.

It's 2AM,

post-another-party.

One in which

we arrived too

in matching royal blue –

a sign?

A sign of our synchronicity?

We decide,

we leave the drunkards

to their games,

and I'm oblivious

to the fact

that we're about to play

one of our own.

Outside,

despite it being so late,

or so early,

there's warmth –

a magic of summer,

you're my

midsummer

night's

dream

but no potion

can solve our problem –

we must talk.

So we walk.

It's blocks

and blocks

before either of us

ever really say anything.

We go to Fran's.

Tightly-packed

though it may be,

it's open

twenty-four hours.

Over my plate

of my pancakes

and your platter

of your waffles,

you finally ask,

What are we to you?

Time cannot stand still —

logically.

Yet,

it does.

Even those around us

seem to cease.

A third bomb

in our already

overwhelmed village.

Tick, tick.

What is the answer

you're hoping for?

Which wire

should I cut?

Is it the red one,

or the blue one?

Like a mathematical exam,

there is only

one correct answer.

Because there is

an answer

that means

this is over.

I have to choose.

Tick, tick.

'You know what we are.'

I play it safe.

But I need

to hear you say it.

You volley it back

with a quickness

that gives me

no time to think.

I think,

I say,

'We are…

friends…

with benefits… '

Tick, tick.

Even as I say it,

I am unsure,

and when I watch

your face slip,

I become sure

I said the wrong thing.

You nod in agreement,

though.

So,

Boom.

Now,

we really talk.

Don't we?

Do you have

just one friend

with benefits

at a time?

What's this?

Follow up

instead of fallout?

Wire or no wire,

I am weary

of this aftershock.

It's a weird one,

I realize,

both the friends

and the benefits

are plural,

or can be,

plural.

What does it mean?

That *S*?

'What do you think?'

This one is yours.

Your answer disappoints.

My face

must've slipped,

but only for the

same second.

We are mirror images

of a moment.

Time is no longer frozen.

It wasn't what I was hoping,

but seems we've met

our quotient for words

that go spoken.

When we leave

that downtown

dine-in spot,

we don't take

our problems

to go.

Our rules then:

be safe

be honest.

We have nothing to hide...

We are lighter,

maybe because we are defined —

a definition of us exists,

even if the exact meaning

is the exact opposite

of what exists

inside our exasperated hearts.

Number Five: I Got… Adventure.

Adventure is a code name

for another man.

This isn't revenge,

or spite —

it's not even curiosity.

What is one to do

with a newfound sense of freedom

if not embrace it?

So off I go,

on adventure.

Adventure is six feet tall,

bearded,

European.

He likes whisky and cigars.

He knows about art.

He compares me to a '69 blend

and to Arturo Fuente

and to The Lady with Fan.

See,

you have to understand.

What we have

is different to you and I —

it's the same lust,

but it's lust

without connection.

Freedom?

Yes,

I guess.

It wasn't anything special

that he said;

maybe I still had

your words in my head,

but your words

weren't the thing

that led me to his bed.

I 've got a problem

with impulse control;

I've gotta fulfill
a desirous soul.
Me and adventure
share time
and have fun.
No seriousness,
no weight,
none.
We do
new activities
that feel like
a fast run.
There's no way
for me
to become undone.
He could've been anyone,
so long as he didn't feel
like a tonne –
the way you do.

Life moves

so very fast

during this

adventurous stint,

so fast, in fact,

I have to

squint while I sprint.

Freedom?

Yes,

I guess.

In between adventures,

when you and I meet,

you say the right things

and you show great support,

you want me to go out there

and you want me to flirt.

You think I need

more experience –

some part of me

is furious,

because as you say

what you say,

the opposite of the truth,

I can see you

judging me,

becoming a sleuth.

You have roundabout ways

of asking about adventure,

but that's a risky venture.

Now,

you want to share

your own other adventures

with me,

but I didn't ask.

Out comes my mask,

since you want to

keep me in the loop.

I jump through hoops,

lying.

'Cool,'

I'll say,

determined

not to become prey –

at your mercy again.

Back up

and reverse.

Everything inside of me

becomes adverse.

I cannot listen to this,

I must disperse.

What's worse?

What curse?

Of all the people

in the universe,

I had to get you –

sweet and sharp

in the same course.

Adventure peaks,

and only after

a few weeks.

Eventually,

I want to stop

adventuring,

because even a fun thing

can become a drain.

Adventure comes

and goes,

but still you remain.

And off,

and off,

it goes,

without any pain.

There's no detonation

or ignition;

there's no spark

as it ends.

When it's time,

it's just a fizzle.

Am I so wrong

for missing the sizzle?

It makes me wonder

and I have to contend.

Did I make a mistake

for agreeing

to be your friend?

In so many ways,

you unleashed me

to the world,

yet,

simultaneously,

you've chained me

with your emotional shackles.

It's a crackle

that becomes the first pop –

we are building toward

a blow and a drop.

You keep me meekly

and you let me go weakly.

How are you in me

so deep and completely?

Number Six: I Got... Novelty.

Novelty is a code name

for another 'nother man.

Novelty is also six feet tall

and bearded –

a pattern, a type, emerges –

except he's large and cuddly

and all he does is work.

Novelty is serious.

Novelty never laughs at himself.

He does not give in

to the folly of emotional expression.

Even when he asks me questions,

he's a surgeon,

looking for an ail,

already prepared

with a solution in mind –

but he can't see it,

it's not written in Braille.

That's the thing
about Novelty.

It is a certainty.

Novelty is a man
who knows what he wants.

A relationship,

a marriage,

multiple children—

I told you he was serious.

And Novelty thinks
he wants those things
with me.

But he doesn't know
that when you call me
at 2AM,

I condemn myself
and I come.

In more ways than one.

All of this mayhem,

all of them,

they stem from you –

I'm a fatale femme

to these men.

But not in your eyes.

You see me as I was before.

Novelty looks forward

but it's in a direction

I don't want to go.

Under his lead,

I freeze.

This should be a breeze.

I should be at ease.

My feelings aren't these.

Please,

he begs,

please.

I want to appease,

but he doesn't make me

weak in the knees.

I know he'll think I'm a tease.

But I am thinking of you.

Novelty is serious

and he's sincere.

He wants me

to tell him my fears.

He wants me

to show him real tears.

He wants us to move

from 4th to 5th gear —

all clear,

full steam ahead.

No, wait.

You're in the way.

Again.

Serious and sincere.

Serious and sincere

are two words

I wouldn't use

to describe you.

Still,

I am drawn to you,

to the idea of us.

Maybe it's the challenge,

maybe that's your talent.

Cause even when you're ungallant,

I come for you.

Novelty asks

and I have to say no.

Novelty asks me

to meet his friends.

Novelty asks me

to meet his family.

Novelty asks to fly me

around the world.

Novelty asks me

to be his girl.

Anyone who juggles long enough

is bound to drop a ball:

Hunger cramp.

Tired arms.

Weak eyes.

I can't keep up

the guise much longer.

Soon enough,

he or I,

will become stronger —

The ball rolls away.

If I picked it back up,

I'd have to start again,

for God's sake,

so I leave it on the ground

and I take a break

from Novelty.

Number Seven: I Got... Romance.

Romance felt a little different

than the others

before him.

First of all,

yes,

he was plus six feet.

And yes,

his beard covered half his face.

He had charm.

He had wit.

He held my attention.

He approached me

with no apprehension,

yet he was a gentleman.

You taught me better,

but still I pretended –

or worse,

I fooled myself –

into thinking

he wanted more

than he wanted.

His approach was different

than yours,

different than

the others.

He reminded me

of passion –

not a lustful passion,

but a passion for love.

He loved love,

and I loved listening to him

lament about love.

He was cupid.

Fingers pinched on the bow's string,

stretching back,

he aimed it

at me.

Fire!

Burning fire.

I didn't know

how to class it,

but he set me

aflame.

I forgot about you.

I wanted to burn

with Romance

until the end of my days,

live under his gaze,

listen to his praise,

suffocate in his haze –

blaze, baby, blaze.

What came with Romance

but bouquets of flowers?

The usual red roses

which were staples of love.

Never mind a dozen,

I got two;

never mind red,

Romance called them rouge.

He promised to pluck me

the rarest flower

in the world, a

 Middlemist's Red,

and when he said promise,

I said yes.

What came with Romance

but dimly lit candles?

Mood-setting,

coquetting,

he'd let them burn

for hours.

Temperature rising,

tranquilizing,

these were Romance's powers.

It was more

than I could have anticipated

and everything I'd awaited.

I didn't yearn for you,

because Romance kept me satiated.

What came with Romance

but fancy dinners?

Five star,

three-course,

exclusive,

lavish,

eclectic.

I had it all.

I got to dress up

in my fanciest shawl,

wear lipstick

too expensive to repeat

and strut around

with red bottoms

on my feet.

It was fantasy

existing in the real,

and when it came to Romance,

I was a hamster to a wheel.

And just when I accepted

romance equalled love…

I learned there were lessons

I was not above.

I learned what Romance

was really capable of.

The Roman god of love

was somewhat of a trickster.

He wanted to leave me

a drifter,

a bitter spinster.

And it was

much too late

when I realized

I had not been shot

by Cupid's arrow,

no,

but by the sharp end

of a plain dart.

A piercing sting

through this

ever weakening heart.

A sinister game,

it is,

one where points

are counted and calculated.

But I participated.

I was drawn

to the flame –

the flame is ember –

and ember becomes ashes.

What can burn forever?

Time:

I thought he and I

had all the right stuff.

I got out in time,

but not in time enough.

Number Eight: I Got... To Stop.

No more code names.

No more them's.

When I'm with them's,

you stay with me.

So there's no point.

But I'm on point

when I say…

I had to stop.

'Cause my current path

was a fruitless one.

It left me feeling

hurt and hollow.

An empty space inside;

without real

significance or value.

Hollow,

like the Borrowdale Yews

or the Marten Oak.

Some trees

are more prone to hollowing,

and I wonder

if people

are like this too.

More likely to give way

from the pressures

and the blues.

Trees hollow

from stress

and from damage –

and that feels

too familiar.

I used to be full,

more than just

the outline of a figure.

So I had to stop

before I withered

into a whisper.

I knew I was a roar.

So I had to stop.

I shouldn't have listened

to you

when you said go,

I should've shouted

and said no.

I shouldn't have listened

to you

when you said freedom,

I should've known

the likely outcome.

I shouldn't have listened

to you

when you said friend,

I should've brought it all

to an end.

Now,

I'm stopping,

but it's late.

You'll be my karma

and that's my fate.

You'll be my karma;

you'll be an answer.

An answer for

my reckless heart,

an answer in a dharma:

I know that

you're my karma.

I know the

things I've done.

I know that

this will be brutal.

But I dare you,

bring it on.

I know that

you're my karma.

I know the

things I've done.

I know you

think you see right through me.

You look at me

with indifferent transparency.

I know that

you're my karma.

I know the

things I've done.

I know you've already

swam in me,

but you have yet to find out

about the hurricane

that I can be.

I know that

you're my karma.

I know the

things I've done.

I know you'll be

the river of tears

I've eluded crying,

but if it's time,

I'm ready

to stop trying.

I know that

you're my karma.

I know the

things I've done.

I know that

this will be brutal.

But I dare you,

bring it on!

I've stopped,

though I'm ready

for whatever truth comes next—

I've stopped.

So that I could still.

So that I could rise again.

My experiences,

my experiences

outside of you,

were everything

under the sun.

Fun,

hard,

gratifying,

indulgent,

painful,

and perhaps most of all,

insightful.

Full,

because I rise still.

I can reset,

step back

from the cheap thrills,

reveal a new will,

standstill.

From the top,

I see my life

as I want it.

And

It's

Still

You.

Why?

My spirit is on fire.

And yours is cool as ice.

And my heart

always seemed untameable.

And yours is locked away tight.

What a pair we'd make,

what a disaster

waiting to happen.

But I'd stay with you.

Like anchors.

In the eye of the storm.

In the belly of the beast.

Where it's quiet.

Where,

somehow,

you make sense to me.

So I hope.

A hope that has

feathers and wings.

A hope that

floats and wheels.

A hope that

forces me to move.

And backwards

is a direction

I can't willingly go again.

I have to know.

If the conscious part of me

refuses to admit

what my subconscious knows,

that you are special,

that you are exactly

what I needed at exactly

this point in my existence,

know that I do know.

For a very,

very long time,

something in me

went to sleep.

I wasn't wallowing

or waiting...

but something was

absent

inside of me.

The thing that made

all my friends

jump from lily pad

to lily pad,

that made them careless

with their croaks,

that ultimately

made them

metamorphose

into their full complete selves

did not exist

inside of me.

I wasn't scared

or sequestering myself.

Something was just

dead or asleep

inside of me.

You took that thing

and you sparked it.

While I wouldn't wish anyone

the absence of that thing,

I pray you get to know

the awakening.

The rebirth.

The thing inside

that demands growth,

demands passion,

demands vulnerability,

came alive again.

I won't let her die again.

I won't even let her sleep again.

You took me

from my timid ways

and introduced me the game.

I know it's good as it is,

and I always hated change.

Except when.

When we are alone.

I have to know.

Your eyes...

Your voice…

Your lips...

Your arms...

Inadequate words!

You trap, consume, liberate,

then condemn me.

But I will have you now.

Will you have me?

For the final time,

I have to know.

Number Nine: I Got... A Friend With Benefits,

Nothing Without.

I inhale,

deep,

stretching my lungs

to their limits,

as if it's the last breath

I'll ever take.

'I love you.'

My voice gives out at the end.

Could you hear me?

Every part of me trembles,

like a shelter dog

who knows it's about to be

put down.

Could you hear me?

You feel so distant to me.

Come back.

I reach out for you

but you're just beyond my grasp.

I hold you too tightly,

and like sand in palms,

you slip away.

Love?

The sound of your scoff

is worse than a death sentence,

and I know,

immediately I know,

you are my executioner.

It doesn't seem to matter,

whether I'm cold as a hockey rink

or soft as Egyptian cotton,

you'd never stay,

you'd never stay,

you'd never stay —

It's me.

I must be malfunctioning,

somehow,

like a clock

that doesn't tick,

or a faucet that doesn't run,

I don't serve my purpose.

Lips pressed together

and doors with no locks

and coffins underground —

I'm sealed.

Yet every single time

you spoke to me,

every single time,

you managed to coax me,

to convince me to part my lips,

to build locks with keys,

to rise from the dirt,

to open.

To you.

For you.

You'll be the one who opens me,

who loves me,

who stays.

Lies.

Beautiful, sweet,

beautiful, brutal

lies.

When you thought

you knew me,

when you had a picture

of who you thought I'd be,

you wanted in.

But I didn't live up

to your impossible,

to your perfect picture

of me.

How?

How do you do it?

How do you make me feel

like I'm not me enough?

On a better day,

I might tell you

to screw yourself.

But today,

today,

I'm not me enough —

and we both know it.

Your words will ring

in my ears,

bells that become deafening

on days like today.

Today,

your words rain down on me

like pellets of ice,

golf balls of hail.

You say,

I think you're an angel.

Me?

Are you joking

with this verbosity?

Me?

Who you know curses,

who you know lies,

who you know cheats.

Me?

Who you plan to walk away from —

what sane person

would leave the light of an angel?

So, you lie,

I think you're too giving.

This was a lesson

I thought I'd already learned.

Yet,

here I am,

learning it again.

I already know a person can,

in fact,

be too giving,

give too much.

Too much of the things

we can't get back.

Energy, and time.

But these are excuses.

More excuses.

Rise up,

like you forced me to,

and tell the truth.

It's me.

 But I just don't have

the time for this,

you say instead.

Ah.

I know this speech well.

I see through

your smoke and mirrors.

You think I'm wonderful,

but…

And is there a worse conjunction

than *but*?

Because that but,

those three letters,

render everything before it

inadmissible,

like faulty evidence

in a courtroom trial.

I'm not wonderful,

or you'd stay.

I'm not some angel,

or you'd never walk away.

The deceit in everything before the

but

breaks me.

I can only hear

everything that follows

after it.

Was it not you

who pursued me?

You who slithered your way

into whatever cracks of time

I could give you?

It was you.

I was fine

before you went and

decided you were the one

who could open me,

who would love me,

who would stay.

Excuses and lies.

Honestly,

you don't have the time

for this anymore

because you're doing

someone else

now.

That's the truth.

The truth that would make you

look like the bad guy

and the truth that would

set me free.

Free from thinking

of all the ways

I disappointed you

by not being me enough.

I was pathetic last time;

I couldn't possibly be pathetic

this time too—

Let him go, please,

I plead with myself,

please,

let him go.

Let him go with grace.

And when you do it,

Look him in the face.

Unafraid.

Unflinching.

And I do.

Or I try.

But before I can,

I remind you,

you're making a gigantic mistake,

because with everything at stake:

I would have been

good to you.

For I was realistic

about you.

I knew you weren't perfect;

I knew you had

shortcomings and faults.

I hoped our imperfections

were compatible ones.

I was at least willing

to give it a real shot,

but at the first sign

of a bump in the road,

a blemish in reality,

you run.

You bolt like Usain.

Cut like Casper.

You don't understand this disaster.

My life has been a home for ghosts,

a place where people passed through

without thanking the host.

I chased shadows

and monsters and memories,

Even without evidence, I could've

searched for centuries.

But not today, I won't beg them to stay,

I realize with every passing breath –

There's no honour in leaving,

no, there's no honour in death.

So,

with benefits came friendship.

But it's RIP to all that.

You stole it all away

with your little coup d'etat.

It's over, it's done,

I'm left with zilch, zero,

nothing and no one.

Number Ten: I Got... To Be Alone.

Every morning

that I wake up,

there's a grace period

where I forget,

or don't remember,

that I'm experiencing

a sort of death.

Then,

it rushes in at once,

seeping into me,

sinking me,

like the Titanic.

So,

of course,

a dream dies with you.

Another future lost

to a blackened ocean.

Another no.

But you were never mean.

Despite its ending,

Despite the hurting,

when reality that it would

never be more glided in,

reared its hideous head,

you were never mean.

You softened my heart

only to take a chunk of it

with you

when you went.

Like a thief

in the night,

you stole something

from me.

You took off

without a proper goodbye.

You are another person

I will have to make peace with.

A small loss

in the grand scheme.

A universe

flashing in and out

of existence

in a nanosecond.

It wasn't

knock your socks off,

homerun,

infinity

type love.

But I can count it

as a sort of love.

I waited. And—

A sort of love came,

and a sort of love left.

And again,

I know you were

another lesson

I was meant to learn.

You ready me

for something deeper.

You make me intentional.

You know what they say

about parting? –

How parting is such sweet sorrow.

Sweet sorrow.

Oxymoronic.

I used to think it was.

But now…

I get it.

Instinctually,

I know you were important.

The same way I knew,

instinctually,

you were impermanent.

Because even though

it feels like

I've been run over

by an eighteen-wheeler,

I know we weren't

meant to be

each other's passengers

for life.

You left me

like you came to me –

unexpectedly.

What an intense

and underappreciated privilege

it is to be alone,

to be in one's own company.

Even if it was suddenly,

even if it wasn't really up to me –

I've found it

to be a privilege.

An immense moment

of reflection,

I add you to my collection.

This quiet,

this peace,

this.

This is what I should've

been chasing.

I have it now,

I've got it,

it's mine.

And I'll have this knowledge

until the end of my time.

My time.

You weren't

the lasting love

that I was hoping for.

But you were

good enough love.

Good enough friendship.

Good enough benefits.

Thank you.

Signed,

Your Old Friend… with Benefits

Fin.

ABOUT THE AUTHOR

Bianca Perrie was born in Toronto, Canada. She holds a Bachelor of Arts degree in English Literature and a Bachelor of Education degree. When she's not writing about love, she's reading romantic novels, watching romantic movies and/or binging any TV series with a will-they-won't-they couple. Her other faves include coffee, wine, chocolate, and puppies.

MORE BOOKS BY BIANCA PERRIE

Printed in Great Britain
by Amazon

84162897R00072